# Absurdle

## THE BOOK THAT MUCKS WITH YOUR HEAD

# Absurdle

## THE BOOK THAT MUCKS WITH YOUR HEAD

## WITH YOUR HEAD

**DK**

# Absurdle

Well, that's what everybody calls it

| S | H | I | R | T |
| P | E | S | T | O |
| B | A | S | S | Y |
| A | S | D | A | S |

| Q | W | E | R | T | Y | U | I | O | P |
| A | S | D | F | G | H | J | K | L |
| ENTER | Z | X | C | V | B | N | M | ⌫ |

# Absurdle

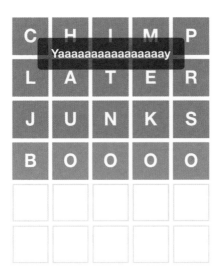

CHIMP
Yaaaaaaaaaaaaaaaay
LATER
JUNKS
BOOOO

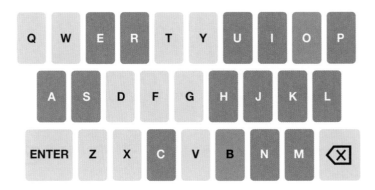

# Absurdle

P R O S E
E B O N Y
G E O I D
G E O F F

Classic lad, Geoff

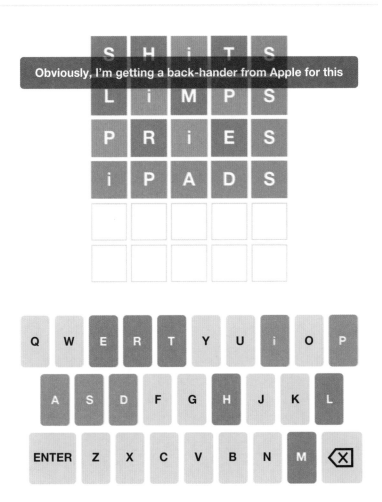

# Absurdle

Respect bruv

CREAM
LUNGS
PINKO
INNIT

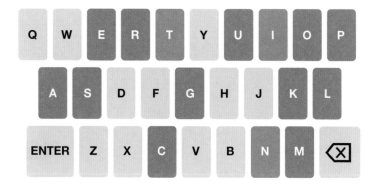

# Absurdle

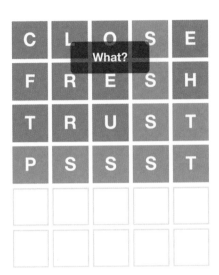

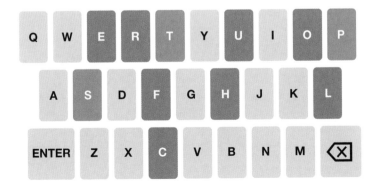

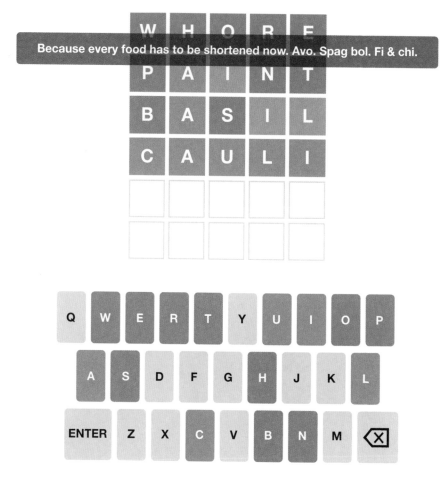

# Absurdle

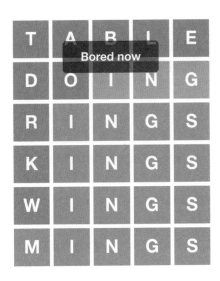

| T | A | B | L | E |
| D | O | I | N | G |
| R | I | N | G | S |
| K | I | N | G | S |
| W | I | N | G | S |
| M | I | N | G | S |

Bored now

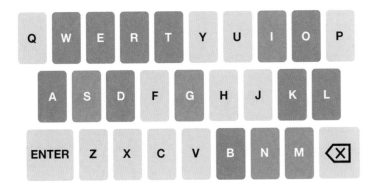

Q W E R T Y U I O P
A S D F G H J K L
ENTER Z X C V B N M ⌫

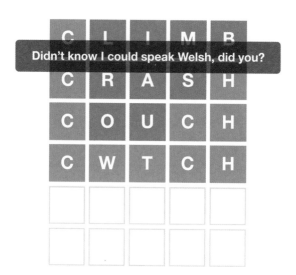

# Absurdle

Didn't know I could speak Welsh, did you?

| C | L | I | M | B |
| C | R | A | S | H |
| C | O | U | C | H |
| C | W | T | C | H |

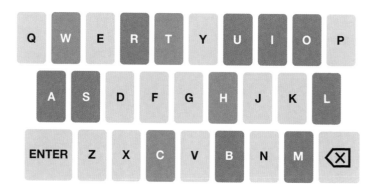

# Absurdle

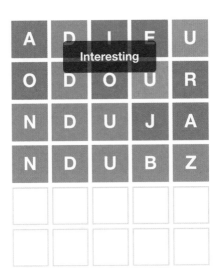

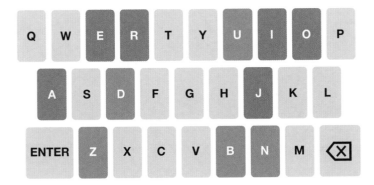

# Absurdle

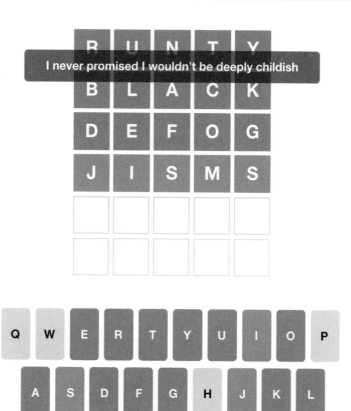

I never promised I wouldn't be deeply childish

# Absurdle

L A N C E

Six goes? Really? When yesterday's word was HOITY?

S H O U T
F O R T Y
M O N T Y
P O T T Y
T O I T Y

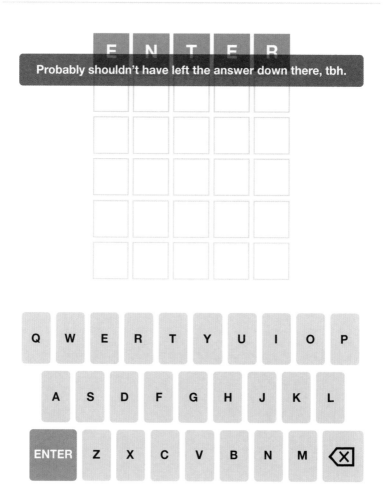

# Absurdle

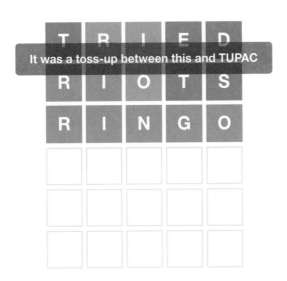

It was a toss-up between this and TUPAC

Grid rows:
- T R I E D
- R I O T S
- R I N G O

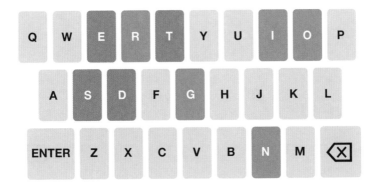

Keyboard:
Q W E R T Y U I O P
A S D F G H J K L
ENTER Z X C V B N M ⌫

# Absurdle

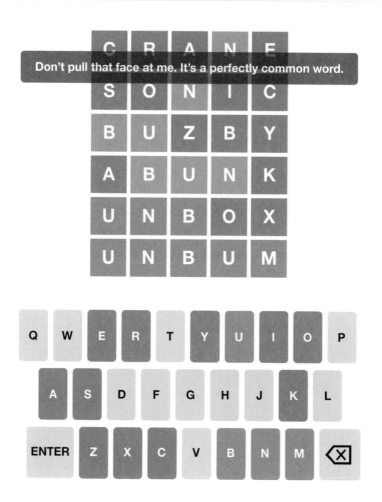

CRANE

Don't pull that face at me. It's a perfectly common word.

SONIC

BUZBY

ABUNK

UNBOX

UNBUM

# Absurdle

D A L E K

Bellend

D R W H O

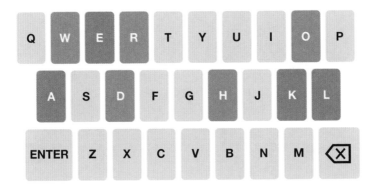

# Absurdle

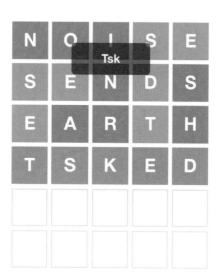

N O I S E
S E N D S
E A R T H
T S K E D

# Absurdle

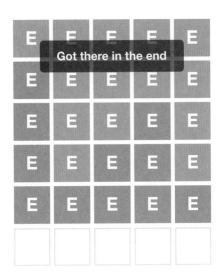

Got there in the end

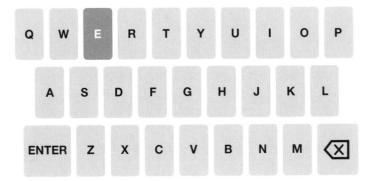

# Absurdle

I've seen your search history, mate

| S | L | A | T | E |
| R | O | L | L | S |
| G | U | L | F | S |
| M | I | L | F | S |

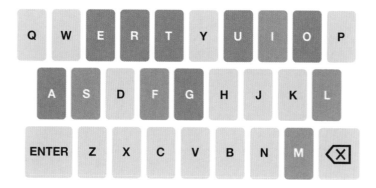

# Absurdle

L O F T Y

Shakespeare probably came up with it

R O F L S

# Absurdle

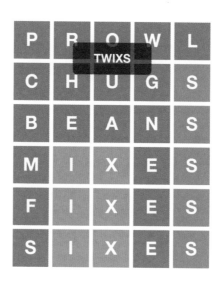

| P | R | O | W | L |
|---|---|---|---|---|
| C | H | U | G | S |
| B | E | A | N | S |
| M | I | X | E | S |
| F | I | X | E | S |
| S | I | X | E | S |

TWIXS

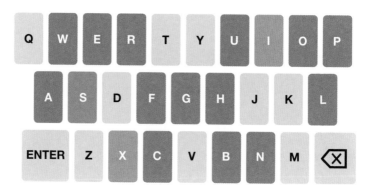

# Absurdle

C I A M P
Everyone's a critic
S H I R T
S H I T E

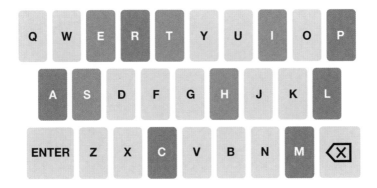

# Absurdle

It's the American spelling

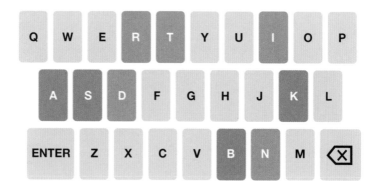

# Absurdle

M U R K Y

Ironically, that was sooo slooooow

D R E A M

P R I S M

B R O O M

G R O O M

V R O O M

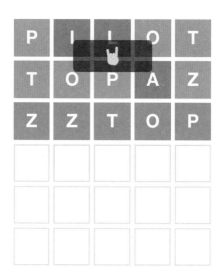

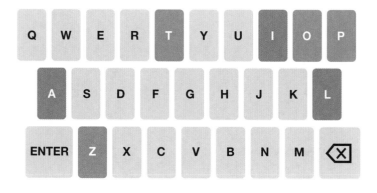

# Absurdle

F E A S T

Could murder a Mivvi right now

J U M B O

M I V V I

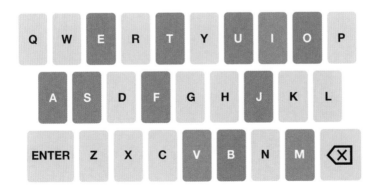

# Absurdle

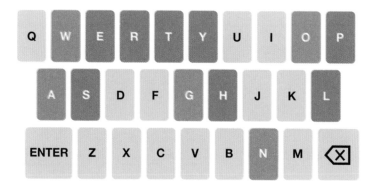

# Absurdle

LEANT
Yes yes yes yes
REBUS
YESES

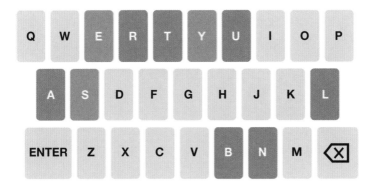

# Absurdle

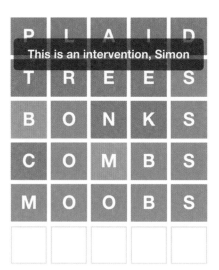

This is an intervention, Simon

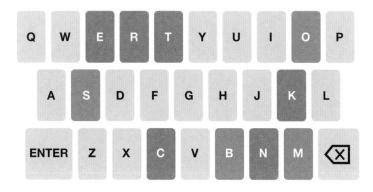

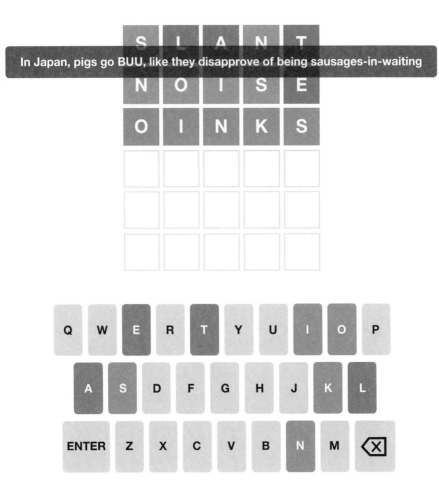

# Absurdle

H O R S E
Sweeeeeeeeeet
C H A N G
G A N J A

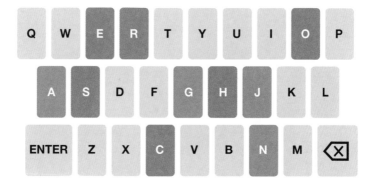

# Absurdle

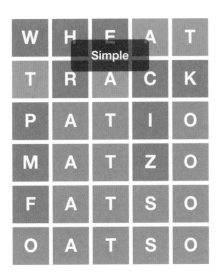

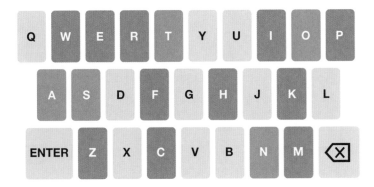

# Absurdle

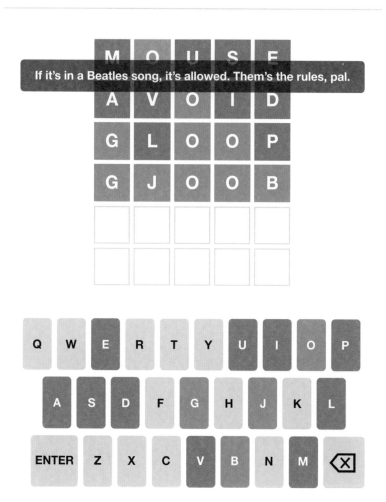

M O U S E

If it's in a Beatles song, it's allowed. Them's the rules, pal.

A V O I D

G L O O P

G J O O B

# Absurdle

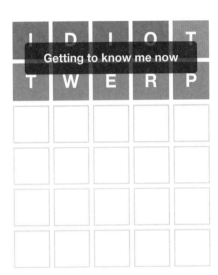

I D I O T

Getting to know me now

T W E R P

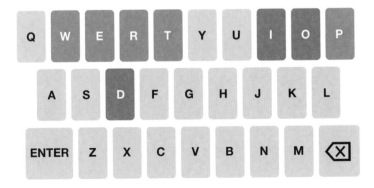

**Absurdle**

S L A N T

This one goes out to all the Lauras

A M P U L

L A U G H

L A U R A

# Absurdle

P L A I D

*If I want an ampersand, I'll bloody well have one*

T H Y M E

T R O T S

T S & C S

# Absurdle

T I D E S

The opposite of which is, of course, FFFIT

C H A M P

F L O U R

F U G L Y

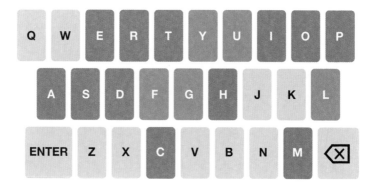

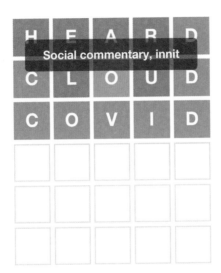

# Absurdle

| H | E | A | R | D |
|---|---|---|---|---|

Social commentary, innit

| C | L | O | U | D |
|---|---|---|---|---|

| C | O | V | I | D |
|---|---|---|---|---|

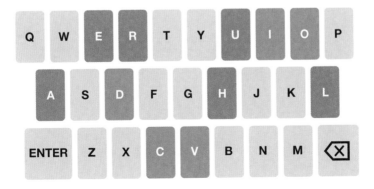

# Absurdle

DEPOT
LEGOS
RECON
SEROW
AESOP
MEMOS
KENOS

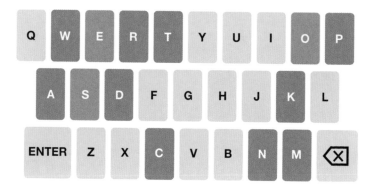

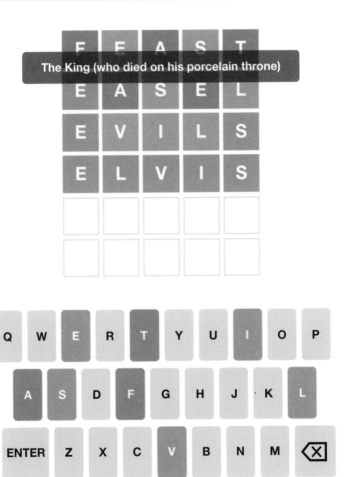

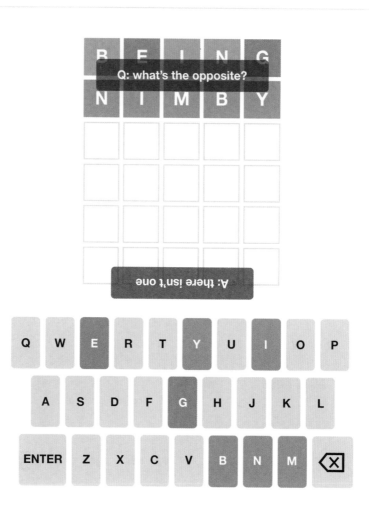

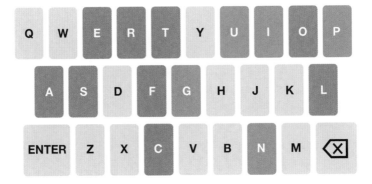

# Absurdle

W H I S T

**Your move**

R U G B Y

J E

N

G A

# Absurdle

# Absurdle

If I had a 10x10 grid, I'd go for MERCEDESES

| F | O | R | D | S |
| A | U | D | I | S |
| S | E | A | T | S |
| S | A | A | B | S |

# Absurdle

Old skool

| A | L | T | E | R |
|---|---|---|---|---|
| M | U | S | I | C |
| B | I | N | G | O |
| P | I | N | K | Y |
| N | I | N | N | Y |
|   |   |   |   |   |

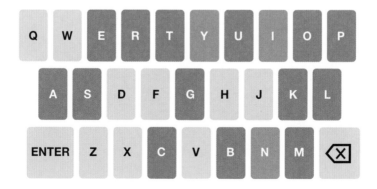

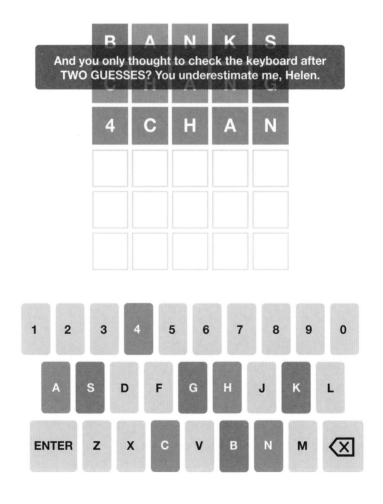

# Absurdle

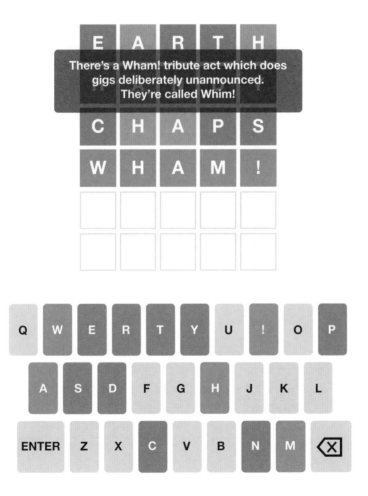

There's a Wham! tribute act which does gigs deliberately unannounced.
They're called Whim!

E A R T H

C H A P S

W H A M !

# Absurdle

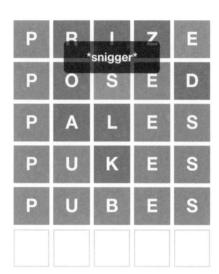

*snigger*

| P | R | I | Z | E |
| P | O | S | E | D |
| P | A | L | E | S |
| P | U | K | E | S |
| P | U | B | E | S |
|   |   |   |   |   |

# Absurdle

I blame that eleven-bean cassoulet

# Absurdle

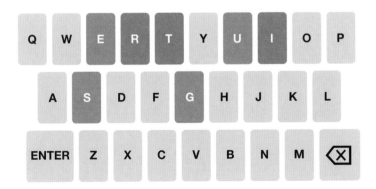

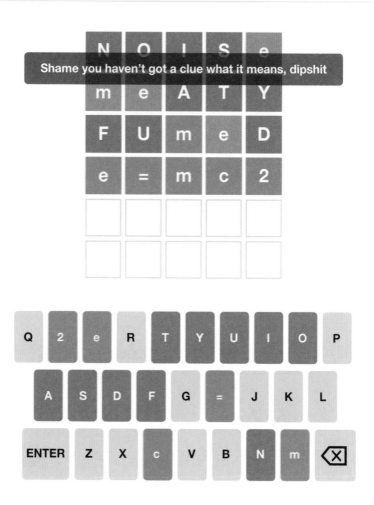

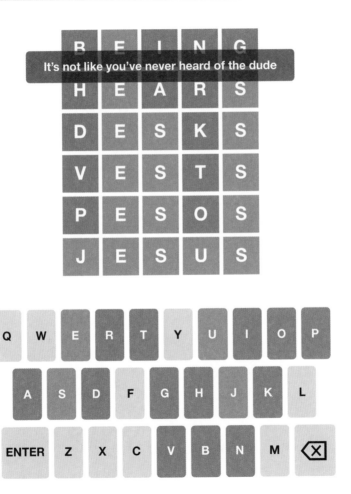

# Absurdle

| A | C | T | E | D |
|---|---|---|---|---|

There's one in that book and another on Top Gear. That's two of them.

| T | H | I | N | G |
|---|---|---|---|---|
| G | R | I | S | T |
| S | T | I | G | S |

| | | | | |
|---|---|---|---|---|
| | | | | |

| Q | W | E | R | T | Y | U | I | O | P |
|---|---|---|---|---|---|---|---|---|---|

| A | S | D | F | G | H | J | K | L |
|---|---|---|---|---|---|---|---|---|

| ENTER | Z | X | C | V | B | N | M | ⌫ |
|---|---|---|---|---|---|---|---|---|

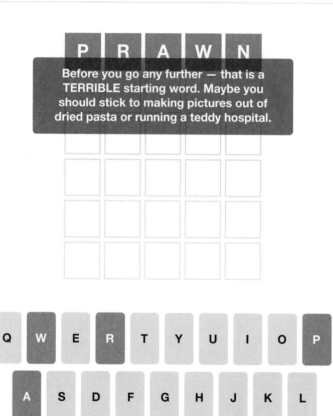

# Absurdle

**P R A W N**

Before you go any further — that is a
TERRIBLE starting word. Maybe you
should stick to making pictures out of
dried pasta or running a teddy hospital.

# Absurdle

| C | H | A | I | N |
|---|---|---|---|---|

Bypassed HANKY and PANKY and went straight for the tugular

| W | A | N | E | D |
|---|---|---|---|---|
| W | A | N | T | S |
| W | A | N | K | Y |
|   |   |   |   |   |
|   |   |   |   |   |

| Q | W | E | R | T | Y | U | I | O | P |
|---|---|---|---|---|---|---|---|---|---|

| A | S | D | F | G | H | J | K | L |
|---|---|---|---|---|---|---|---|---|

| ENTER | Z | X | C | V | B | N | M | ⌫ |
|-------|---|---|---|---|---|---|---|---|

# Absurdle

PLEBS, you pleb

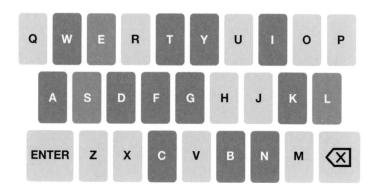

# Absurdle

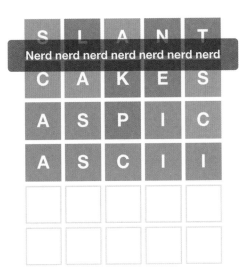

S L A N T
Nerd nerd nerd nerd nerd nerd nerd
C A K E S
A S P I C
A S C I I

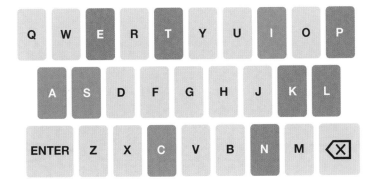

# Absurdle

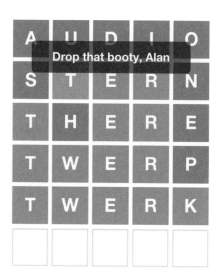

Drop that booty, Alan

| A | U | D | I | O |
| S | T | E | R | N |
| T | H | E | R | E |
| T | W | E | R | P |
| T | W | E | R | K |

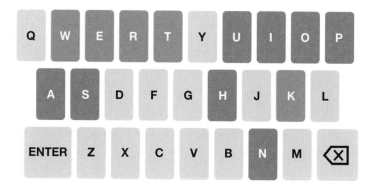

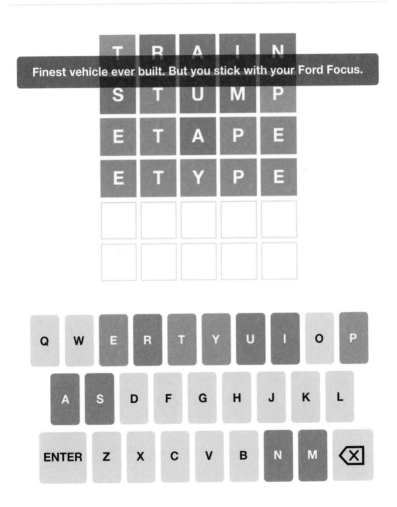

# Absurdle

T R A I N

**Finest vehicle ever built. But you stick with your Ford Focus.**

S T U M P

E T A P E

E T Y P E

Q W E R T Y U I O P

A S D F G H J K L

ENTER Z X C V B N M ⌫

# Absurdle

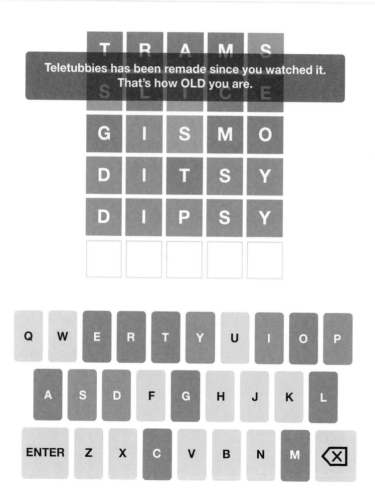

T R A M S

Teletubbies has been remade since you watched it.
That's how OLD you are.

S L I C E

G I S M O

D I T S Y

D I P S Y

# Absurdle

| D | E | P | O | T |
|---|---|---|---|---|

**GLANS**

| S | L | A | I | N |
|---|---|---|---|---|

| C | L | A | M | S |
|---|---|---|---|---|

**That's right: GLANS**

| F | L | A | W | S |
|---|---|---|---|---|

| B | L | A | H | S |
|---|---|---|---|---|

| P | L | A | N | S |
|---|---|---|---|---|

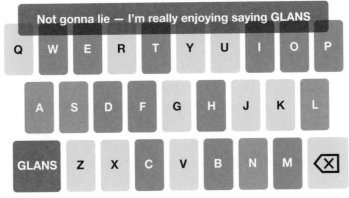

**Not gonna lie — I'm really enjoying saying GLANS**

| Q | W | E | R | T | Y | U | I | O | P |
|---|---|---|---|---|---|---|---|---|---|

| A | S | D | F | G | H | J | K | L |
|---|---|---|---|---|---|---|---|---|

| GLANS | Z | X | C | V | B | N | M | ⌫ |
|---|---|---|---|---|---|---|---|---|

# Absurdle

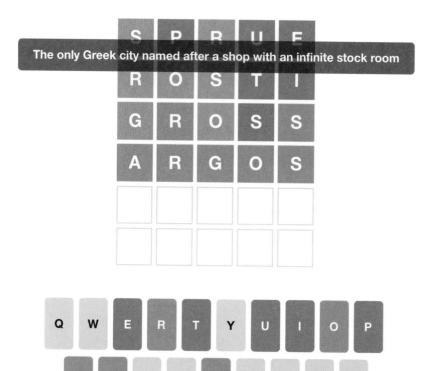

The only Greek city named after a shop with an infinite stock room

S P R U E

R O S T I

G R O S S

A R G O S

# Absurdle

Flybe next

| C | L | O | W | N |
| N | A | M | E | S |
| M | A | N | L | Y |
| P | A | N | A | M |

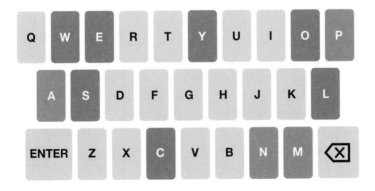

# Absurdle

Enjoy your earmworm, sucker

D R E A M
M A C A W
Y M C A S

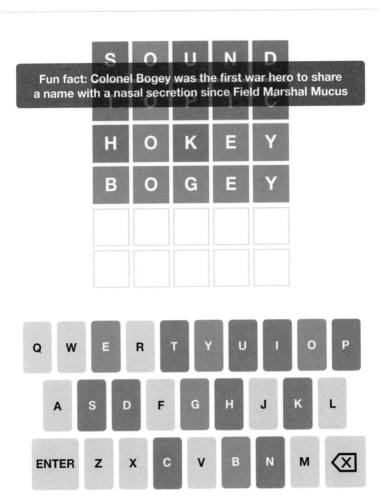

# Absurdle

S O U N D

**Fun fact: Colonel Bogey was the first war hero to share a name with a nasal secretion since Field Marshal Mucus**

T O P I C

H O K E Y

B O G E Y

# Absurdle

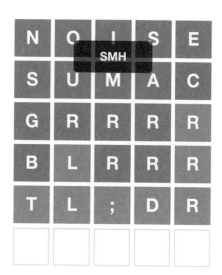

| N | O | I | S | E |
| S | U | M | A | C |
| G | R | R | R | R |
| B | L | R | R | R |
| T | L | ; | D | R |

SMH

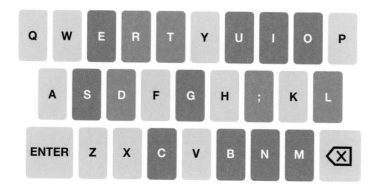

# Absurdle

L A U G H

Jewellery to you, dinosaur

G L I N T

B L I N G

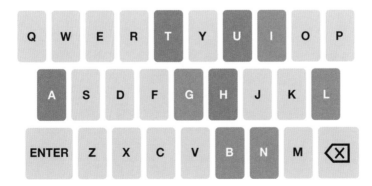

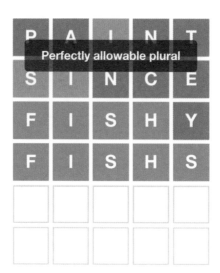

Absurdle

Perfectly allowable plural

# Absurdle

S P I C Y

You've unlocked one of the forbidden characters. #EndOfLevel

C H A S M

R O C K S

F A C E S

F Æ C E S

# Absurdle

| I | N | T | R | O |
|---|---|---|---|---|

COMPO, you 1W bulb. Yesterday's was CLEGG. I mean, I do try.

| B | A | N | J | O |
|---|---|---|---|---|
| G | O | N | Z | O |
| L | O | T | T | O |
| F | O | R | G | O |
| P | O | L | I | O |

| Q | W | E | R | T | Y | U | I | O | P |
|---|---|---|---|---|---|---|---|---|---|
| A | S | D | F | G | H | J | K | L |
| ENTER | Z | X | C | V | B | N | M | ⌫ |

# Absurdle

Aiming way too high, frankly

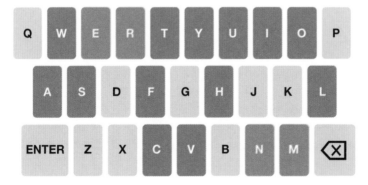

# Absurdle

It's one of the classic words

| B | E | A | M | S |
|---|---|---|---|---|
| S | K | I | N | T |
| S | P | O | O | F |
| S | P | R | U | E |
| S | P | L | U | P |
|   |   |   |   |   |

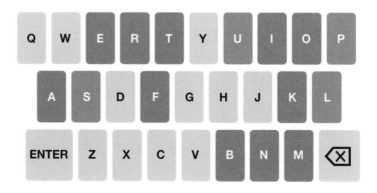

# Absurdle

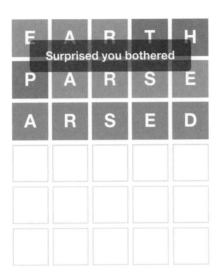

EARTH
Surprised you bothered
PARSE
ARSED

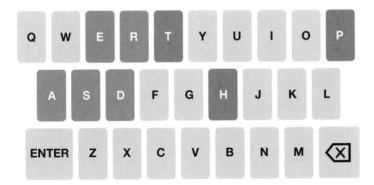

Q W E R T Y U I O P

A S D F G H J K L

ENTER Z X C V B N M ⌫

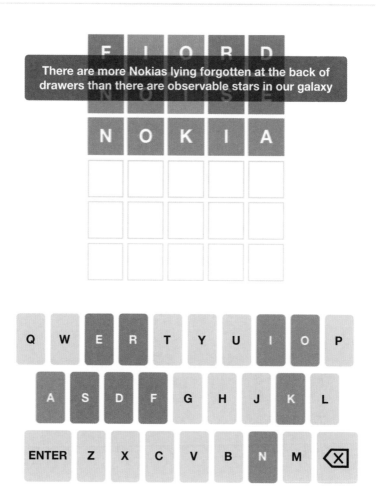

# Absurdle

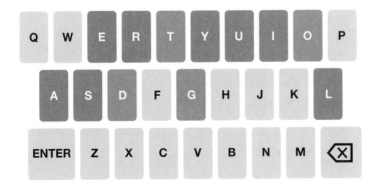

You were never supposed to get that

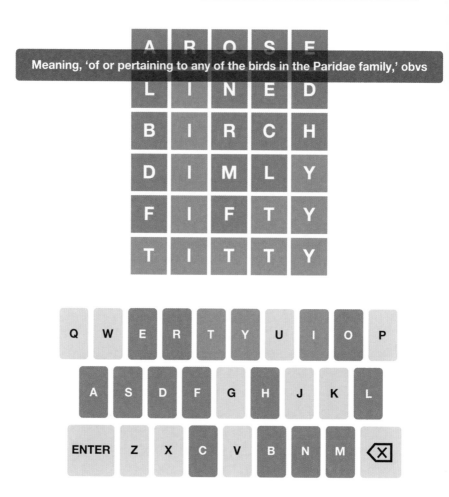

# Absurdle

| A | R | O | S | E |
| L | I | N | E | D |

Meaning, 'of or pertaining to any of the birds in the Paridae family,' obvs

| B | I | R | C | H |
| D | I | M | L | Y |
| F | I | F | T | Y |
| T | I | T | T | Y |

# Absurdle

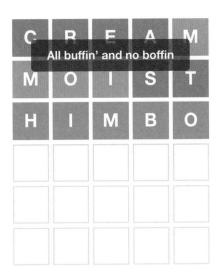

All buffin' and no boffin

| C | R | E | A | M |
| M | O | I | S | T |
| H | I | M | B | O |

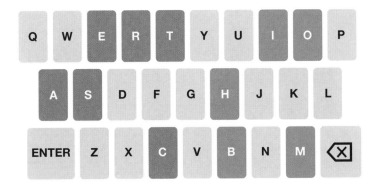

# Absurdle

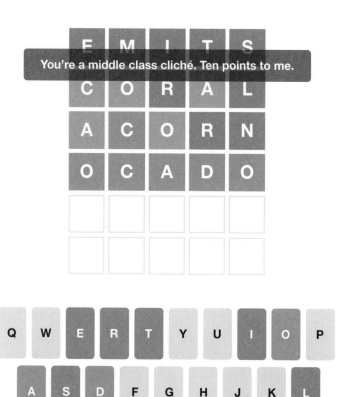

E M I T S

You're a middle class cliché. Ten points to me.

C O R A L

A C O R N

O C A D O

# Absurdle

| T | R | A | D | E |
|---|---|---|---|---|

Natch. How else are you going to describe something uncle-like?

| S | C | I | O | N |
|---|---|---|---|---|

| U | N | C | L | Y |
|---|---|---|---|---|

| Q | W | E | R | T | Y | U | I | O | P |

| A | S | D | F | G | H | J | K | L |

| ENTER | Z | X | C | V | B | N | M | ⌫ |

Look at yourself

# Absurdle

N O I S E
S N O W Y
S N O U T
S N O O P
S N O B S
S N O G S

Phwoargh

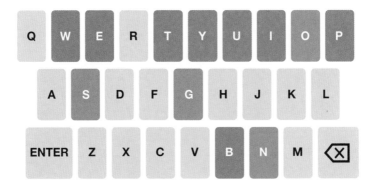

# Absurdle

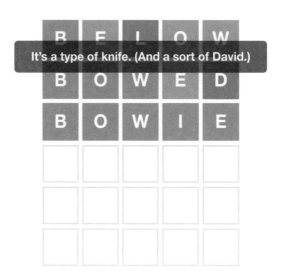

It's a type of knife. (And a sort of David.)

B E L O W
B O W E D
B O W I E

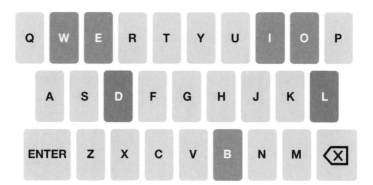

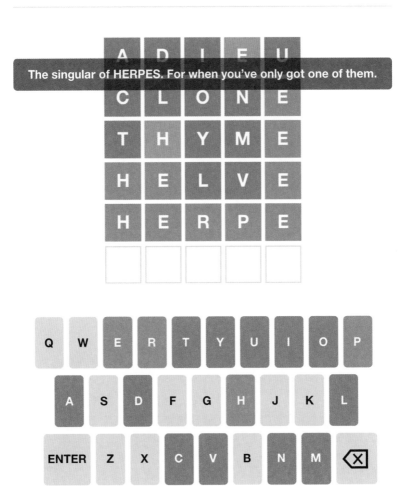

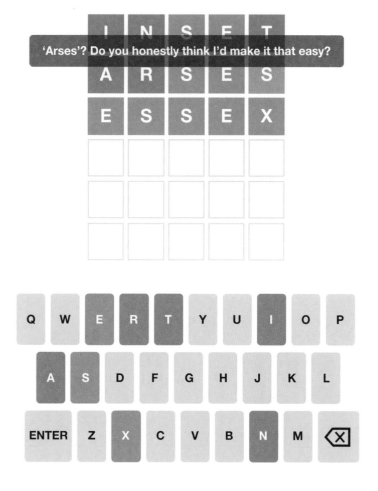

# Absurdle

A U D I O
Your mum
T O A D S
Q A N O N

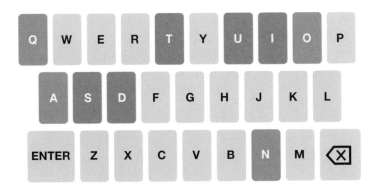

# Absurdle

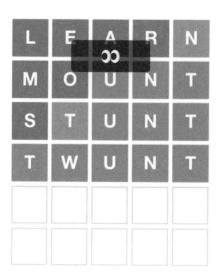

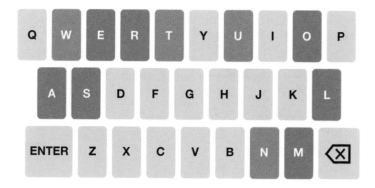

# Absurdle

SINCE
Dahling!
PASTY
FLASK
BOARS
CHADS
MWAHS

CHEAT

You bloody cheat

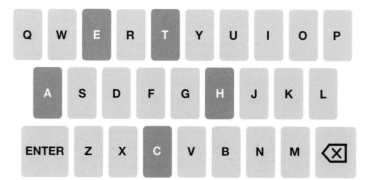

**Aquisitions Editor** Marleigh Price
**Designer** Amy Cox
**DTP and Design Co-ordinator** Heather Blagden
**Production Editor** David Almond
**Production Controller** Samantha Cross
**Art Director** Maxine Pedliham
**Publishing Director** Katie Cowan

First published in Great Britain in 2022 by
Dorling Kindersley Limited
DK, One Embassy Gardens, 8 Viaduct Gardens,
London, SW11 7BW

The authorised representative in the EEA is
Dorling Kindersley Verlag GmbH. Arnulfstr. 124,
80636 Munich, Germany

A CIP catalogue record for this book
is available from the British Library.
ISBN: 9780-2-4161-769-4

Printed and bound in the United Kingdom

## For the curious
**www.dk.com**